SOUPS AND STARTERS

Text by Carolyn Garner
Photography by Peter Barry

1513
This 1992 edition published by Tiger Books International PLC, London
© 1986 Coombe Books
All rights reserved
ISBN 1-85501-226-X

SOUPS AND STARTERS

CAROLYN GARNER

TIGER BOOKS INTERNATIONAL
LONDON

Contents

Introduction

The secret of a great soup or starter is that it should tantalize the tastebuds without satisfying the appetite. When choosing a soup or starter, the main meal and in fact the rest of the menu should be kept in mind. Pay special attention to the presentation as it does a lot to excite the appetite. Avoid a repetition of flavours, colours or textures.

In this book, the quantities given are for starters and for soups eaten at the beginning of a meal. However, a soup may be a meal in itself, served piping hot with fresh bread for supper on a cold wintry night, or chilled for a light lunch on a hot summer's day. For a first course serving of soup, allow about 150-200ml (¼–⅓ pint) per person. Soups are made with a variety of basic and nourishing foods: meat, fish, poultry, vegetables and fruit, and with the addition of many different herbs and spices. Ideally a stock should be used to make most soups and, if time permits, this can generally be used to replace stock cubes. Three basic stocks are brown stock, chicken stock and fish stock.

To make brown stock, brown 1kg (2lbs) of fresh meat bones in the oven. Place the bones, 2 peeled and chopped onions, 2 chopped sticks of celery, 2 chopped carrots, 3 peppercorns, a teaspoon of salt and a bouquet garni in a large saucepan and cover with 2 litres (4 pints) of cold water. Bring to the boil and simmer for 4-5 hours. Skim any scum from surface as necessary. Cool and strain. When cold, remove any fat with absorbent paper or, if solidified, with a spoon.

To make chicken stock, place chicken carcass, bones and any scraps of chicken meat in a large saucepan and add an onion, which has been peeled and chopped roughly, 2 chopped carrots and a bouquet garni. Cover with 1½ litres (3 pints) of cold water. Cover and simmer for about 3 hours. Strain and when cold, remove any fat present.

To make a fish stock, place fish carcass, a diced carrot, a diced leek, a peeled and sliced onion and a bouquet garni in a large pan. Add 1½ litres (3 pints) of cold water, bring to the boil, and simmer for only 30 minutes. Strain.

Stocks will keep for 2-3 days in the refrigerator, and up to a week if boiled up every day. Of course they will keep much longer if frozen. A good soup can be made with left-over vegetables and added to, boiling up each day so that a large pot of soup is available for a few successive days of the week. In fact the flavour usually improves after the soup has been left to infuse overnight.

All the soups in this book and many of the starters require no cooking or can be prepared well ahead of time, thus taking the pressure off the cook when making the final preparations to the main meal. Careful planning will help to ensure the success of the dinner. The prelude should pave the way for what is to follow – a promise of things to come.

Hot Soups

Hot and Sour Seafood Soup

PREPARATION TIME: 20 minutes
COOKING TIME: 20 minutes
SERVES: 4 people

3 dried Chinese mushrooms, soaked
   in hot water for 20 minutes
1 cake fresh bean curd, diced
115g (4oz) prawns or shrimps, shelled
   and de-veined
600ml (1 pint) fish stock
60g (2oz) white fish fillet
15ml (1 tbsp) oyster sauce
15ml (1 tbsp) light soy sauce
15ml (1 tbsp) lemon juice
½ tsp lemon rind, cut into slivers
15ml (1 tbsp) vegetable oil
1 red chilli, seeds removed, and finely
   sliced
1 green chilli, seeds removed, and
   finely sliced
2 spring onions, sliced
Salt
Pepper
1 tsp sesame oil

Garnish
Fresh coriander, if desired

Soak mushrooms in hot water and
set aside. Heat vegetable oil, and
add prawns, chillies, lemon rind
and spring onions. Add stock,
oyster sauce and light soy sauce and
bring to the boil. Reduce heat and
simmer for 5 minutes. Season to
taste. Remove hard stalks from
mushrooms and slice caps finely.
Dice white fish fillets and add them
with bean curd and Chinese
mushrooms to the soup, cooking
for a further 5 minutes. Stir in
lemon juice and sesame oil. Adjust
seasoning, and serve sprinkled with
fresh coriander leaves if desired.

Egg and Lemon Soup

PREPARATION TIME: 15 minutes
COOKING TIME: 15 minutes
SERVES: 4 people

750ml (1¼ pints) chicken stock
30g (1oz) small noodles/soup pasta
2 small eggs, separated
1 lemon
Salt
White pepper
Sugar, if desired

Garnish
Slivers of pared lemon rind

Bring stock to the boil and add the
noodles. Cook for 10 minutes or
until noodles are tender, stirring
occasionally. Meanwhile, juice
lemon, and beat the egg whites
until stiff. Add the yolks and beat

until light and creamy. Add lemon
juice gradually, beating all the time.
Add a cup of the soup to the egg
mixture and whisk. Pour back into
the soup, whisking continuously.
Adjust seasoning to taste. Garnish
with pared lemon rind. Serve
immediately.

**This page: Hot and Sour
Seafood Soup.**

**Facing page: Egg and Lemon
Soup (top) and Celery and
Apple Soup (bottom).**

French Onion Soup

PREPARATION TIME: 15 minutes

COOKING TIME: 1 hour

SERVES: 4 people

*450g (1lb) onions, peeled and sliced
    thinly*
60g (2oz) butter or margarine
45g (1½oz) flour
1 litre (2 pints) boiling water
2 beef stock cubes
1 small French loaf
*30g (1oz) Parmesan or Gruyère
    cheese, grated*
Salt
Pepper

Melt butter in a thick saucepan.
Add onions and cook gently over
moderate heat until golden brown
– about 15 minutes – being careful
not to burn them. Stir occasionally.
Meanwhile, dissolve stock cubes in
boiling water and put aside to cool.
Stir flour into onions and cook for
2 minutes. Add stock gradually,
stirring continuously. Simmer for
30 minutes. Add salt and pepper to
taste. Pre-heat oven or grill. Slice
bread thickly and place in bottom
of ovenproof serving dish. Pour
over soup. Sprinkle the bread with
cheese and place under the grill or
in a hot oven until browned. Serve
very hot.

Tomato Soup

PREPARATION TIME: 15 minutes

COOKING TIME: 45 minutes

SERVES: 4 people

450g (1lb) ripe tomatoes
1 carrot
1 onion
600ml (1 pint) water
1 chicken stock cube
30g (1oz) butter or margarine
30g (1oz) flour
Pinch of grated nutmeg
1 tsp basil
Salt
Pepper

Garnish
Chopped parsley

Peel and finely dice onion and
carrot. Cut tomatoes into quarters
and squeeze out pips into a sieve.

**This page: Goulash Soup
(top) and Curried Chicken
Soup (bottom).**

**Facing page: Tomato Soup
(top) and French Onion Soup
(bottom).**

Strain pips and retain the juice. Melt butter in a pan. Fry the onion and carrot gently until the onion is transparent. Draw off heat and stir in the flour, nutmeg and basil. Add tomatoes, juice and water, return to heat and stir until boiling. Add crumbled chicken stock cube and salt and pepper to taste. Cover and simmer for 30 minutes. Push the soup through a sieve and return to pan. Adjust seasoning and reheat. Garnish with chopped parsley.

Bumper Soup

PREPARATION TIME: 30 minutes

COOKING TIME: 1 hour 45 minutes

SERVES: 4 people

1 litre (2 pints) good beef stock
450g (1lb) spinach, stalks removed, and shredded
2 onions, peeled and diced
2 carrots, scraped and diced
2 potatoes, peeled and diced
3 sticks celery, sliced
1 tbsp chopped parsley
2 tbsps tomato purée
½ cup lentils
Salt
Pepper

Heat stock in pan. When hot, add vegetables, parsley, tomato purée and seasoning. Bring to boil and simmer for 1 hour. Add lentils and simmer for a further 30 minutes stirring occasionally. Adjust seasoning if necessary. Serve hot.

Red Pepper Soup

PREPARATION TIME: 15 minutes

COOKING TIME: 45 minutes

SERVES: 4 people

1 medium onion, peeled and finely chopped
3 tomatoes
3 red peppers
30g (1oz) butter or margarine
1 litre (2 pints) chicken stock
Salt
Pepper

Garnish
Chopped parsley and sliced red pepper

Remove core and seeds from peppers. Slice a pepper for garnish and set aside. Chop remaining peppers and tomatoes into small pieces. Melt butter in a large saucepan and add onion, tomatoes and peppers and fry gently for 5 minutes, stirring continuously. Pour on chicken stock, add salt and pepper and bring to the boil.

Simmer for 30 minutes. Push the soup through a sieve to remove skin and any pips. Adjust seasoning. Add a pinch of sugar if desired. Serve hot or cold, sprinkled with parsley and garnished with a slice of red pepper.

Curried Chicken Soup

PREPARATION TIME: 10 minutes

COOKING TIME: 20 minutes

SERVES: 4 people

30g (1oz) butter or margarine
2 tsps curry powder
1 tbsp flour
1 chicken stock cube
1 litre (2 pints) water
½ tsp paprika
2 tbsps tomato chutney
60g (2oz) cooked chicken, chopped
30g (1oz) rice
Yolk of 1 egg
60ml (4 tbsps) single cream
Salt
Pepper

Garnish
Chopped parsley or coriander

Melt butter in pan. Stir in curry powder and flour. Cook gently for 2 minutes. Draw off heat. Gradually stir in stock cube disolved in water. Add paprika and bring to the boil to thicken. Add chutney, chicken, and rice and simmer for 12-15 minutes. Mix egg yolk with cream and gradually add to soup off the heat. Do not re-boil. Season to taste. Serve hot, garnished with chopped parsley or coriander.

Goulash Soup

PREPARATION TIME: 20 minutes

COOKING TIME:
2 hours 45 minutes

SERVES: 4 people

750g (1½ lbs) skirt or chuck steak, cut into 2.5cm (1") cubes
4 medium onions, peeled and chopped roughly or quartered
1 green pepper, cored, seeds removed, and chopped
4 tomatoes, skinned and quartered
4 tbsps tomato purée
600ml (1 pint) good beef stock
1 tbsp paprika
30g (1oz) butter or margarine
15ml (1 tbsp) oil
450g (1lb) potatoes, peeled and cut into bite-size pieces
15g (½oz) flour
Salt
Pepper

Heat oil in pan. When hot, add steak in batches so as not to overcrowd, and sauté over a high heat until well browned all over. Remove and set aside. Add butter, onion and green pepper, and fry until onion is lightly browned. Stir in flour. Remove from heat. Add stock, return to heat and bring to the boil, stirring continuously. Add tomato, tomato purée, paprika and salt and pepper to taste. Reduce heat, return meat, cover and simmer for 2 hours, stirring occasionally and adding more stock or water if necessary. Add potatoes and cook gently for a further 20 minutes, or until potatoes are cooked through.

Celery and Apple Soup

PREPARATION TIME: 15 minutes

COOKING TIME: 45 minutes

SERVES: 4 people

1 onion, peeled and chopped
3 sticks celery, chopped
3 cooking apples, peeled and sliced
30g (1oz) butter or margarine
1 chicken stock cube
1 litre (2 pints) water
1 bay leaf
1 tbsp cornflour
Salt
Pepper

Garnish
Finely sliced celery

Melt butter in pan. Add onion and fry for 5 minutes, then add apple and a third of the celery, and fry a further 5 minutes. Heat water. Add to crumbled stock cube and pour onto onion/apple mixture. Add salt, pepper and bay leaf. Bring to the boil and simmer for ½ hour. Push through a sieve and then return to the pan. Blend cornflour with a little water, and stir into the soup. Bring soup to the boil, and cook for 2-3 minutes, stirring continuously. Cook remaining celery in water until tender. Add to soup. Garnish with finely sliced celery. Serve immediately.

Minestrone

PREPARATION TIME: 30 minutes

COOKING TIME: 1 hour 15 minutes

SERVES: 4 people

1 carrot, cut into strips
1 leek, sliced
1 turnip, cut into strips
3 tomatoes, skinned and diced
1 stick celery, chopped
4 rashers streaky bacon, blanched and diced
¼ small cabbage, sliced
3 cloves garlic, crushed
1 onion, peeled and sliced
30g (1oz) butter or margarine
1 litre (2 pints) good, fat-free chicken stock
60g (2oz) short-cut or elbow macaroni
Salt
Pepper

Red Pepper Soup (right) and
Bumper Soup (bottom).

Accompaniment
Freshly grated Parmesan cheese, if desired

Melt butter in pan, and add garlic, onion, leek and celery. Cover and cook over a gentle heat for 15 minutes without colouring. Add carrot and turnip, stock, and salt and pepper to taste. Bring to the boil, cover and simmer for 30 minutes. Add cabbage and simmer a further 5 minutes. Add tomato and macaroni, and simmer gently, uncovered, for 15 minutes. Meanwhile, grill bacon until crisp. Serve on top of soup with a side serving of Parmesan cheese if desired.

Cream of Cauliflower Soup

PREPARATION TIME:	10 minutes
COOKING TIME:	45 minutes
SERVES:	4 people

1 cauliflower
60g (2oz) butter or margarine
45g (1½oz) flour
600ml (1 pint) chicken stock
1 onion, peeled and chopped
2 medium egg yolks
150ml (¼ pint) double cream
Cheese, grated
Nutmeg
Salt
Pepper

Garnish
Snipped chives

Trim and break cauliflower into florets. Cook in gently boiling salted water for 5 minutes. Drain and set aside. Melt butter in pan and stir in the flour. Cook for 1-2 minutes, stirring. Remove from heat and stir in chicken stock. Add onion, and return to heat. Bring to

This page: Cream of Cauliflower Soup (top) and Lettuce Soup (bottom).

Facing page: Minestrone.

boil, stirring continuously, and simmer for 20 minutes. Allow to cool. Add cauliflower and blend. Push through a sieve. Return to pan, and re-heat. Lightly beat together egg yolks, cream and grated cheese. Stir in some soup, and then put all of the mixture back into the pan. Cook gently until thickened, but do not let it boil. Season with salt and pepper and grated nutmeg. Garnish with snipped chives.

Watercress Soup

PREPARATION TIME: 15 minutes

COOKING TIME: 45 minutes

SERVES: 4 people

4 bunches watercress, washed and trimmed
1 leek, cleaned and sliced thinly
225g (8oz) potatoes, peeled and sliced thinly
60g (2oz) butter or margarine
600ml (1 pint) chicken stock
Pinch grated nutmeg
45ml (3 tbsps) cream
Salt
Pepper

Garnish
Watercress

Heat butter and slowly soften leek. Add potatoes, stock and seasoning. Bring to the boil and simmer 15 minutes. Add watercress and simmer a further 10 minutes. Blend soup and push through a sieve. Adjust seasoning and add cream. Re-heat or chill as required. Garnish with watercress.

Carrot and Orange Soup

PREPARATION TIME: 15 minutes

COOKING TIME: 40 minutes

SERVES: 4 people

1 onion, peeled and chopped finely
2 carrots, grated
1 strip lemon rind
1 orange
600ml (1 pint) water
1 chicken stock cube
60g (2oz) butter or margarine
30g (1oz) flour
15ml (1 tbsp) cream, if desired
Sugar, salt and pepper to taste
Pared orange rind, cut into fine shreds

Garnish
Carrot flowers

Melt half the butter in pan. Add onion, carrots and lemon rind. Cover and cook until onion is transparent. Push through a sieve and set aside. Pare and shred rind of orange. Squeeze orange. Blanch orange rind in boiling water. Drain and save. Melt remaining butter in the pan and stir in flour. Remove from heat and add water. Return to heat and bring to the boil, stirring continuously. Add crumbled stock cube, orange juice and vegetables. Simmer for 5 minutes, blend and return to pan. Add salt, pepper and sugar to taste. Add cream and orange rind, and stir. Serve garnished with carrot flowers. To make carrot flowers, slice strips out lengthways to produce flower shape when cut across in rounds.

Pumpkin Soup

PREPARATION TIME: 10 minutes

COOKING TIME: 1 hour

SERVES: 4 people

450g (1lb) pumpkin, peeled, seeds removed and diced
30g (1oz) butter or margarine
1 onion, peeled and chopped
1 litre (2 pints) beef stock
30ml (2 tbsps) cream
Pinch of turmeric
Salt
Pepper

Garnish
Croûtons

Melt butter in pan. Add onion and cook over gentle heat until lightly coloured. Add stock and pumpkin. Add salt and pepper and turmeric and bring to the boil. Reduce heat. Cover and simmer for 30 minutes. Purée and push through a sieve. Return to pan and bring to boil. Remove from heat, stir in cream, and serve garnished with croûtons. Serve immediately.

This page: Watercress Soup (top) and Pumpkin Soup (bottom).

Facing page: Pea and Ham Soup (top) and Carrot and Orange Soup (bottom).

To Make Croûtons

Take one slice of bread and cut into 1cm (¼″) cubes. Fry in hot oil until browned well all over. Remove with a slotted spoon and drain on absorbent paper. Sprinkle with salt. Add to soup at last minute otherwise they will go soggy.

Mussel Soup

PREPARATION TIME: 15 minutes
COOKING TIME: 20 minutes
SERVES: 4 people

*2 litres (4 pints) live mussels,
  scrubbed clean
2 onions, peeled and chopped
2 cloves garlic, crushed
2 tbsps chopped parsley
60g (2oz) butter or margarine
300ml (½ pint) dry white wine
30ml (2 tbsps) lemon juice
Salt
Pepper*

Garnish
Chopped parsley

Place mussels, butter, garlic, onions, wine, parsley and a pinch of freshly ground black pepper in a pan, and cover. Place over a high heat and cook for a few minutes. Shake the pan to move the mussels and distribute the heat well. When mussels have all opened, transfer to serving dish and keep warm. Discard any that remain closed. Strain juices and return to pan. Reduce liquid by half over a high heat. Adjust seasoning. Whisk in lemon juice and pour hot soup over mussels. Serve immediately sprinkled with chopped parsley.

Cream of Spinach Soup (left),
Vegetable Soup (below) and
Mussel Soup (facing page).

Cream of Spinach Soup

PREPARATION TIME: 10 minutes
COOKING TIME: 30 minutes
SERVES: 4 people

325g (11oz) packet frozen chopped
    spinach
1 onion, peeled and chopped
30g (1oz) butter or margarine
30g (1oz) flour
900ml (1½ pints) milk
150ml (¼ pint) cream
Pinch of ground nutmeg
Salt
Pepper

Garnish
Cream

Allow spinach to thaw. Drain off excess liquid. Heat butter in pan and fry chopped onion until transparent. Stir in flour and gradually add milk, stirring all the time until thickened. Season with salt and pepper and nutmeg. Stir in spinach and cook for 10 minutes. Stir in all but 15ml (1 tbsp) of cream. Re-heat carefully, do not re-boil. Garnish with remaining cream and serve.

Pea and Ham Soup

PREPARATION TIME: 1 hour
COOKING TIME: 1 hour
SERVES: 4 people

115g (4oz) dried split peas
115g (4oz) tinned shoulder or leg
    ham, diced
30g (1oz) butter or margarine
1 onion, peeled and chopped
600ml (1 pint) chicken stock
2 tbsps chopped mint
1 stick celery, diced
Salt
Pepper

Garnish
Sprig of mint

Cover peas with boiling water, and leave to soak for 30 minutes. Drain and repeat process, and leave for a further 30 minutes. Melt butter in a pan. Add onion and celery and fry gently for 5 minutes or until transparent. Add drained peas, stock, 1 tbsp mint, and salt and pepper, and simmer gently for 45 minutes. Sieve the soup or blend until smooth. Return to pan. Add ham, and remaining mint, and cook for a further 5 minutes. Adjust seasoning. Serve immediately, garnished with a sprig of mint if desired.

Lobster Bisque

PREPARATION TIME: 20 minutes
COOKING TIME: 1 hour
SERVES: 4 people

1 cooked lobster
1 onion, peeled and diced
1 stick celery, cut into 2.5cm (1")
    slices
1 carrot, diced
1 litre (2 pints) fish stock or water
1 bay leaf
6 peppercorns
Parsley stalks
Salt
Pepper
30g (1oz) butter or margarine
30g (1oz) flour
5ml (1 tsp) lemon juice
30ml (2 tbsps) cream
45ml (3 tbsps) white wine
2 tsps tomato purée

Garnish
Soured cream and chopped parsley

Remove meat from body, tail and claws of lobster. Put lobster shell, stock or water, onion, carrot, celery, herbs and seasoning into a pan. Bring to boil and simmer for 45 minutes. Allow to cool. Strain and reserve stock. Meanwhile, cut lobster meat into bite-size pieces. Melt butter in pan, stir in flour, and cook for 1 minute. Remove from heat and stir in reserved stock gradually. Return to heat. Bring to the boil, and simmer for 5 minutes, stirring continuously. Remove from heat and add lemon juice, tomato purée, wine and cream, and whisk in well. Adjust seasoning. Add lobster meat and garnish with soured cream and chopped parsley if desired. Serve immediately.

Lettuce Soup

PREPARATION TIME: 10 minutes
COOKING TIME: 30 minutes
SERVES: 4 people

175g (6oz) lettuce leaves
1 small onion, peeled and diced
30g (1oz) butter or margarine
300ml (½ pint) chicken stock
150ml (¼ pint) milk
60ml (4 tbsps) single cream
½ tsp grated nutmeg
Salt
Pepper

Blanch lettuce leaves in boiling water for 30 seconds. Rinse under cold water and drain well. Chop roughly. Fry the onion in the butter for 5 minutes, or until it is soft. Add lettuce and stock, and bring to the boil. Simmer gently for 10 minutes. Season with nutmeg and salt and pepper. Blend the soup. Add milk and re-heat. Stir in cream and re-heat gently, being careful not to boil the soup. Serve immediately.

Sweetcorn and Bacon Soup

PREPARATION TIME: 10 minutes
COOKING TIME: 20 minutes
SERVES: 4 people

1 onion, peeled and chopped
30g (1oz) butter or margarine
2 tbsps flour
150ml (¼ pint) water
300ml (½ pint) milk
300g (10oz) can sweetcorn
4 rashers bacon, rind removed
Salt
Pepper

Garnish
Chopped chives

Heat butter in pan. Add onion, and fry until transparent. Stir in flour, remove from heat and add water and milk gradually. Return to heat, stirring until thickened. Add undrained sweetcorn to pan, and season to taste. Bring to the boil, and simmer for 10 minutes. Meanwhile, pre-heat grill. Cut rashers in half lengthways and form into rolls. Grill and serve in soup. Garnish with chopped chives.

Vegetable Soup

PREPARATION TIME: 20 minutes
COOKING TIME: 50 minutes
SERVES: 4 people

2 medium onions, peeled and finely
    chopped
1 carrot, finely diced
½ small turnip, finely diced
900ml (1½ pints) beef stock
30g (1oz) butter or margarine
1 leek, cut into small rings
1 tbsp tomato purée
2 tbsps chopped parsley
Salt
Pepper

Garnish
Chopped parsley

Melt butter in a saucepan and add onions. Cook gently over a low heat for 5 minutes or until transparent. Add carrot and turnip, stock, seasoning and parsley. Bring to the boil and simmer gently for 15 minutes. Add leek, and tomato purée and simmer for a further 20 minutes. Garnish with chopped parsley. Serve hot.

Mushroom Soup

PREPARATION TIME: 10 minutes
COOKING TIME: 45 minutes
SERVES: 4 people

225g (8oz) flat or cup mushrooms
1 small onion
45g (1½oz) butter or margarine
45g (1½oz) flour
600ml (1 pint) water
1 chicken stock cube
15ml (1 tbsp) lemon juice
200ml (⅓ pint) milk
1 tbsp chopped parsley
1 tbsp chopped chives
Salt
Pepper

Garnish
Chopped parsley

Melt butter in a pan. Peel and chop onion and fry gently until transparent. Wash, trim and finely slice mushrooms. Add to pan and cook for 5 minutes, stirring often. Stir in flour and cook for 1 minute. Draw off heat and gradually add water. Return to heat and bring to boil, stirring continuously. Add crumbled chicken stock cube and stir until soup has thickened. Add lemon juice and milk. Cover and simmer for 15 minutes. Add chives and parsley and season with salt and pepper. Garnish with chopped parsley.

Facing page: Mushroom Soup (top) and Sweetcorn and Bacon Soup (bottom).

Fish Soup

PREPARATION TIME: 15 minutes

COOKING TIME: 40 minutes

SERVES: 4 people

1kg (2lbs) of sea-bass, whiting,
    monkfish and/or John Dory, skin
    and bones removed, and cut into
    bite-size pieces
2 onions, peeled and chopped
3 cloves garlic, crushed
2 tomatoes, skinned and chopped

15ml (1 tbsp) oil
Sprig of fresh thyme
1 bay leaf
2 pieces thinly pared orange rind
150ml (¼ pint) dry white wine
Salt
Pepper

Garnish
Chopped parsley

Make a court bouillon with the
heads and trimmings of fish, one-
third of the onion and 1 litre
(2 pints) of water. Simmer 15
minutes, then strain. Put oil in a
heavy pan and heat gently. Add
garlic and remaining onion. Cover
and fry gently for 5 minutes
without colouring. Add fish,
tomatoes, herbs, orange rind, wine,
salt and pepper and court bouillon.
Bring to boil and simmer for 10
minutes. Remove bay leaf, thyme
and orange rind. Serve hot,
sprinkled with parsley.

**This page: Fish Soup (top)
and Lobster Bisque (bottom).**

**Facing page: Avocado Cream
Soup (top) and Tomato and
Cucumber Soup (bottom).**

Cold Soups

Tomato and Cucumber Soup

PREPARATION TIME:
20 minutes, plus chilling time

SERVES: 4 people

6 tomatoes, skinned
2 large cucumbers, peeled and cut
* into pieces, reserving 5cm (2") at*
* end for garnish*
45ml (3 tbsps) lemon juice
150ml (¼ pint) soured cream
1 onion, peeled and grated
1 tsp tomato purée
Salt
Pepper

Garnish
Cucumber slices

Chop tomatoes. Remove pips. Strain juice, and discard pips. Put tomato flesh and juice, cucumber, onion, tomato purée and lemon juice into a blender. Blend at high speed for a few minutes until smooth. Stir in soured cream, and salt and pepper to taste. Serve chilled, garnished with cucumber slices.

Prawn and Cucumber Soup

PREPARATION TIME:
20 minutes, plus chilling time

SERVES: 4 people

450g (1lb) prawns, cooked, shelled
* and de-veined*
200g (7oz) cream cheese
1 small cucumber
½ tsp dry mustard
Salt
White pepper
150ml (¼ pint) single cream
300ml (½ pint) milk

Garnish
Finely sliced cucumber
Dill

Finely chop prawns. Peel and slice cucumber. Place prawns, cucumber, mustard, white pepper and a pinch of salt in a bowl. Beat cream cheese until soft and creamy, and gradually add cream and milk. Add cucumber and prawn mixture, and blend thoroughly. Cover and chill. If

Avocado Cream Soup

PREPARATION TIME:
10 minutes, plus chilling time

SERVES: 4 people

300ml (½ pint) good, fat-free chicken
   stock
2 ripe avocados
15ml (1 tbsp) lemon juice
150ml (¼ pint) milk
150ml (¼ pint) single cream
Salt and white pepper

Garnish
Snipped chives, if desired

Peel avocados, remove seeds, chop
and put in blender with cream,
lemon juice and milk, and blend
until smooth. Put avocado mixture
and chicken stock in a bowl, and
stir until combined. Push through a
sieve. Season with salt and white
pepper. Chill in refrigerator.
Garnish with chives, if desired.

Raspberry Soup

PREPARATION TIME:
5 minutes, plus chilling time

COOKING TIME: 20 minutes

SERVES: 4 people

225g (8oz) raspberries, fresh, or
   frozen and thawed
30ml (2 tbsps) lemon juice
45ml (3 tbsps) sweet sherry
30g (1oz) granulated sugar
300ml (½ pint) single cream
300ml (½ pint) water
Crushed ice

Put sugar, raspberries, lemon juice,
sherry and water in a pan, and heat
gently for 10 minutes. Bring to the
boil and simmer for 5 minutes.
Remove from heat and push
through a sieve, and allow to cool.
Stir in cream. Chill. Serve with
crushed ice.

necessary, thin soup further with
milk. Garnish with sliced cucumber
and dill.

Blackberry and Apple Soup

PREPARATION TIME:
5 minutes, plus chilling time

COOKING TIME: 30 minutes

SERVES: 4 people

450g (1lb) blackberries, fresh, or
   frozen and thawed
2 apples, skinned, cored and sliced
60g (2oz) granulated sugar
600ml (1 pint) water
Crushed ice

Place apples and water in a pan and
bring to the boil. Simmer covered
for 15 minutes until apples are
softened. Add sugar and blackberries, and simmer a further
15 minutes. Purée and push
through a sieve. Chill. Serve with
crushed ice.

Rhubarb Soup

PREPARATION TIME:
15 minutes, plus chilling time

COOKING TIME: 20 minutes

SERVES: 4 people

450g (1lb) rhubarb, trimmed and cut
   into 2.5cm (1") lengths

2 tbsps redcurrant jelly
60g (2oz) granulated sugar
300ml (½ pint) orange juice
300ml (½ pint) water

Garnish
Slivered, pared rind of orange

Place rhubarb, redcurrant jelly,
sugar and water in pan. Cover and
heat gently for 10 minutes. Add
orange juice and bring to the boil.
Simmer uncovered for 5 minutes.
Remove from heat, and allow to
cool. Purée or push through a sieve,
and chill. Serve garnished with
slivered orange rind and crushed ice
if desired.

Blackberry and Apple
Soup (left), Rhubarb
Soup (centre), Raspberry
Soup (bottom) and
Prawn and Cucumber
Soup (facing page).

Vichyssoise (Leek and Potato Soup)

PREPARATION TIME:
15 minutes, plus chilling time

COOKING TIME: 30 minutes

SERVES: 4 people

3 large leeks
2 medium potatoes, peeled and sliced
   thinly
1 small onion, peeled and sliced
30g (1oz) butter or margarine
600ml (1 pint) boiling water
½ chicken stock cube
150ml (¼ pint) single cream
Salt
White pepper

Garnish
Parsley or chives

Wash and trim leeks, discarding roots and any green part. Slice thinly. Melt butter in pan and add leek and onion. Cover, and allow to sweat gently over low heat for about 10 minutes. Dissolve ½ chicken stock cube in boiling water. Add potatoes to leek and pour over the stock. Season to taste. Cover and cook for a further 15 minutes, or until potatoes are soft. Push through a fine sieve. Cool. Stir in cream. Adjust seasoning. Chill well for at least 2 hours. Serve garnished with parsley or snipped chives.

Gazpacho

PREPARATION TIME:
20 minutes, plus chilling time

SERVES: 4 people

450g (1lb) ripe tomatoes, skinned
   and roughly chopped
1 onion, peeled and diced
1 green pepper, cored, seeds removed,
   and diced
Half a cucumber
2 tbsps stale white breadcrumbs
2 cloves garlic, crushed
30ml (2 tbsps) red wine vinegar
1 large can tomato juice
Salt
Pepper

Accompaniments
Diced cucumber, onion, tomato and
   green pepper

Soak breadcrumbs in vinegar. Reserve tomato flesh, and half the onion and half the green pepper for garnish. Blend remaining onion and remaining green pepper with tomato juice, breadcrumbs, vinegar, and garlic, and season to taste.

Push through a sieve. Chill well. Meanwhile, skin and chop cucumber. Serve with crushed ice and small bowls of cucumber, onion, tomato and green pepper.

Beetroot Soup

PREPARATION TIME:
10 minutes, plus chilling time

COOKING TIME: 1 hour 15 minutes

SERVES: 4 people

450g (1lb) raw beetroot
1 shallot, peeled and quartered
2 tbsps sugar
15ml (1 tbsp) lemon juice
Bouquet garni
1 litre (2 pints) water
1 chicken stock cube
Salt
Pepper

Bring water to boil. Peel and dice beetroot. Add to water with crumbled stock cube, shallot, bouquet garni, sugar, lemon juice

and salt and pepper. Bring to the boil. Reduce heat, and simmer, uncovered, for about an hour. Blend and push through sieve and leave to cool. When cool, put into refrigerator to chill.

Beetroot Soup (left) and Vichyssoise (Leek and Potato Soup) (bottom).

Pâtés and Dips

Tzatziki (Cucumber and Yogurt Salad)

PREPARATION TIME: 15 minutes
SERVES: 4 people

1 cucumber, peeled
1 clove garlic, crushed
1 medium-sized carton plain yogurt
10ml (2 tsps) lemon juice
1 tsp chopped mint
Salt

Garnish
Cucumber slices
Sprig of mint

Grate the cucumber and drain off any excess liquid. Mix cucumber with garlic and yogurt. Stir in lemon juice and mint, and add salt to taste. Garnish with a few cucumber slices and a sprig of mint.

Taramasalata (Cod Roe Salad)

PREPARATION TIME: 30 minutes
SERVES: 4 people

225g (8oz) smoked cod roe
½ onion, peeled and grated
2 cloves garlic, crushed
115g (4oz) white bread, crusts
*   removed*
60ml (4 tbsps) milk
90ml (6 tbsps) olive oil
30ml (2 tbsps) lemon juice
Pepper

Garnish
Lemon
Parsley

Crumble bread into a bowl, and add milk. Leave to soak. Scoop the cod roe out of its skin and break it down with a wooden spoon. Squeeze bread dry in a sieve. Add onion, garlic and bread to cod roe,

This page: Taramasalata (Cod Roe Salad) (top) and Tzatziki (Cucumber and Yogurt Salad) (bottom).

Facing page: Gazpacho

and mix well. Very gradually add oil and lemon juice, alternating between the two. Beat until smooth and creamy. Add pepper to taste, and salt if necessary. Garnish with lemon and parsley, and serve with Melba toast (see recipe for Guacamole) or sliced French loaf, and unsalted butter.

Crudités with Anchovy Dip, Oxford Dip, and Tomato and Chilli Dip

Crudités
Half a cauliflower, broken into florets
Half a cucumber, cut into batons
115g (4oz) button mushrooms, cleaned
3 carrots, scraped and cut into sticks
8 small radishes, cleaned
1 red pepper, cored, seeds removed, and cut into strips
8 spring onions, trimmed
2 courgettes, cut into strips

Anchovy Dip
45g (1½ oz) can anchovy fillets, drained and mashed
2 cloves garlic, crushed
30g (1oz) butter or margarine
150ml (¼ pint) double cream, lightly whipped
1 tsp marjoram or oregano
1 tsp chopped fresh parsley
Pinch sugar or salt, to taste

Melt butter in pan, add garlic, and cook for 1 minute. Add anchovies, herbs and sugar or salt to taste. Cook for 10 minutes, stirring continuously. Set aside. When cool, fold in whipped cream. Chill.

Oxford Dip
Pared rind of 1 lemon
5ml (1 tsp) lemon juice
1 tsp English mustard
½ tsp grated root ginger
2 tbsps redcurrant jelly
60ml (4 tbsps) red wine
1 tsp arrowroot

Blanch rind in boiling water for 30 seconds. Remove and shred finely. Put all ingredients except wine and arrowroot into a pan, and bring to the boil, stirring continuously. When mixed, stir in wine and simmer, uncovered, for 15 minutes. Slake arrowroot in 15ml (1 tbsp) of water and add to pan. Simmer a further 3 minutes, stirring continuously. Chill.

Tomato and Chilli Dip
400g (14oz) can plum tomatoes, drained, reserving juice, and pips removed
1 red chilli, seeds removed, sliced finely

1 clove garlic
1 onion, peeled and chopped finely
15ml (1 tbsp) lemon juice or white wine vinegar
1 tbsp chopped fresh parsley
15g (½ oz) butter or margarine
Salt
Pepper

Melt butter in pan. Add garlic and fry until browned. Discard garlic. Add onion and cook gently till softened. Add chilli and cook a further 3 minutes. Add tomatoes, lemon juice or vinegar, reserved tomato juice and salt and pepper and simmer gently for 10 minutes. Remove from heat and set aside to cool. Push through a sieve, stir in parsley, and chill.

Pâté aux Herbes

PREPARATION TIME:	20 minutes
COOKING TIME:	1 hour
OVEN TEMPERATURE:	170°C; 350°F; Gas Mark 2
SERVES:	4 people

450g (1lb) pork, finely minced
325g (11oz) packet frozen spinach
225g (8oz) rashers of streaky bacon, rind removed
1 onion, peeled and chopped
2 cloves garlic, crushed
2 tbsps finely chopped fresh basil
2 tbsps chopped parsley
Freshly grated nutmeg
Freshly ground black pepper
½ tsp sage
1 can leg or shoulder ham
1 egg, lightly beaten
Pinch of cayenne pepper
150ml (¼ pint) double cream
Salt

Cook spinach in boiling salted water for 5 minutes. Drain and press between two plates to remove excess water. Chop finely and mix with pork. Combine onion, garlic, herbs and spices, cayenne pepper, cream, and salt and pepper. Cut ham into strips. Line bottom and sides of ovenproof tureen with rashers of streaky bacon. Mix pork and spinach into cream mixture. Add egg and stir thoroughly. Press one-third mixture into tureen. Add half the ham strips. Repeat until all ham and mixture is used up. Cook in a slow oven for 45 minutes. Remove from oven, cool, and serve sliced.

Guacamole

PREPARATION TIME:	15 minutes
COOKING TIME:	5 minutes
SERVES:	4 people

2 ripe avocados
15ml (1 tbsp) lemon juice
1 clove garlic, crushed
1 red chilli, seeds removed, sliced finely
1 shallot, very finely chopped, or grated
¼ tsp ground chilli powder
Pinch of paprika
Salt

Garnish
Lemon slices and parsley
Serve with melba toast if desired

Blanch chilli and shallot in boiling water for 2 minutes. Drain and set aside. Peel the avocados. Pierce the skin with the point of a sharp knife and run down from top to bottom of the pear in quarters. Pull skin back off fruit and remove stone from centre and any dark bits of flesh. Mash the flesh to a purée and mix in lemon juice. Stir in garlic and shallot. Add chilli, chilli powder, paprika and salt, a bit at a time, to desired taste. Garnish with lemon and parsley. Serve with Melba toast if desired.

Melba Toast
Pre-heat grill. Put slices of bread in toaster and toast until golden brown. Remove crusts and cut horizontally through toast whilst still hot. Cut into triangles and toast untoasted side under the grill until golden brown. Keep inside a clean tea-towel until ready to serve.

Crudités (right) with Anchovy Dip (bottom), Oxford Dip (far right) and Tomato and Chilli Dip (below).

Tomato, Carrot and Spinach Slice

PREPARATION TIME:
30 minutes, plus chilling time

SERVES: 4 people

*6 tomatoes, skinned, with pips
   removed*
450g (1lb) spinach, cooked
Pinch of nutmeg
3 carrots, finely grated
*150ml (¼ pint) double cream,
   whipped*
11g (⅓ oz) gelatine

60ml (4 tbsps) water
Salt
Pepper

Grease and line a loaf tin with greaseproof paper. Blend tomato in a food processor until smooth. Add salt and pepper to taste. Set aside. Put water in a small bowl. Sprinkle over gelatine and leave 15 minutes to soak. Place bowl in a saucepan of hot water, so that water is part way up side of bowl. Heat gently until gelatine has dissolved. Meanwhile, chop spinach, squeeze out excess liquid and stir in half the cream. Add nutmeg, and salt and pepper to taste. Set aside. Stir one-third of gelatine into tomato mixture, and return bowl of gelatine to saucepan. Fill tomato into loaf tin. Level out, and put into freezer compartment. Leave 10 minutes. Meanwhile, stir carrot and remaining cream together. Stir half of remaining gelatine into carrot mixture, and pour over tomato mixture. Return tin to freezer for 10 minutes. Stir remaining gelatine into spinach mixture, and pour onto carrot layer. Smooth out and put into freezer for a further 10 minutes. Remove from freezer and chill in refrigerator overnight.

This page: Tomato, Carrot and Spinach Slice.

Facing page: Salmon, Watercress and Tomato Slice (top) and Pâté aux Herbes (bottom).

Salmon, Watercress and Tomato Slice

PREPARATION TIME: 30 minutes

SERVES: 4 people

6 tomatoes, skinned, and pips
   removed
Half a bunch of watercress
225g (8oz) can red or pink salmon
150ml (¼ pint) double cream,
   whipped
11g (⅓ oz) gelatine
60ml (4 tbsps) water
Salt
Pepper

Garnish
Watercress

Grease and line a loaf tin with
greaseproof paper. Drain, and place
salmon and one-third of the cream
into a food processor, and process
until smooth. Add salt and pepper
to taste. Set aside. Put water in a
small bowl, and sprinkle over
gelatine. Leave 15 minutes to soak.
Place bowl in a sauepan of hot
water so that water is partway up
side of bowl. Heat gently until
gelatine has dissolved. Meanwhile,
chop watercress, squeeze out excess
liquid, and stir in half the remaining
cream. Add salt and pepper to
taste. Set aside. Place tomatoes and
remaining cream in food processor,
and process. Stir one-third of
gelatine into tomato mixture and
return bowl of gelatine to saucepan.
Fill tomato into loaf tin. Level out,
and put into freezer compartment
for 10 minutes. Stir half the
remaining gelatine into watercress
mixture and pour over tomato
mixture. Return tin to freezer for
10 minutes. Stir remaining gelatine
into salmon mixture and pour onto
watercress layer. Smooth out and
put into freezer for 10 minutes.
Remove from freezer and chill in
refrigerator overnight. Garnish with
watercress.

Salmon Pâté

PREPARATION TIME: 15 minutes

SERVES: 4 people

225g (8oz) can red or pink salmon,
   drained
115g (4oz) curd cheese
30g (1oz) butter
Pinch of ground mace or ground
   nutmeg
Few drops of lemon juice
¼ tsp tabasco sauce
30ml (2 tbsps) double cream
Salt
Pepper

Garnish
Gherkins (slice each gherkin
   horizontally 4 or 5 times, and splay
   into a fan)

Remove any bones from salmon.
Work into a paste with the back of
a spoon. Cream the butter and
cheese until smooth. Add salmon,
lemon juice, seasonings and cream,
and mix well. Put into a large dish
or individual ramekins. Garnish
dish with a gherkin fan.

Chicken Liver Pâté

PREPARATION TIME: 15 minutes

COOKING TIME: 15 minutes

SERVES: 4 people

225g (8oz) chicken livers, trimmed
1 onion, peeled and diced finely
30g (1oz) butter for frying
60g (2oz) butter, creamed
1 clove garlic, crushed
15ml (1 tbsp) brandy
5ml (1 tsp) Worcestershire sauce
Salt
Pepper

Garnish
Dill

Heat butter in frying pan. Add
garlic, onions, salt, and freshly
ground black pepper, and fry gently
until onions have softened.
Increase heat, and sauté chicken
livers in hot butter for about
2 minutes on each side, until just
cooked through. Add Worcestershire sauce and stir. Blend contents
of frying pan and push through a
wire sieve with the back of a spoon
into a bowl. Beat in creamed butter,
brandy, and adjust seasoning. Place
in one large dish or individual
ramekin dishes. If not being eaten
straight away, seal surface with
clarified butter and refrigerate.
Garnish with dill.

Smoked Mackerel Pâté

PREPARATION TIME:
30 minutes, plus chilling time

SERVES: 4 people

225g (8oz) smoked mackerel fillets,
   skinned and bones removed
60g (2oz) butter
Juice of half an orange
1 tsp tomato purée
5ml (1 tsp) white wine vinegar
Black pepper, freshly ground
Salt, if desired

Garnish
1 can pimentos

Aspic
300ml (½ pint) clear, strained
   chicken stock
2 tsps powdered gelatine
30ml (2 tbsps) dry sherry
30ml (2 tbsps) cold water
or
1 packet commercial aspic, used as
   directed

Cream butter. Place butter, smoked
mackerel, orange juice, tomato
purée, vinegar and black pepper in
a blender. Blend until smooth. Add
salt if necessary. Place in one dish or
individual dishes. Cut pimentos
into strips. Sprinkle gelatine over a
small bowl with 15-30ml (1-2 tbsps)
of cold water in it and leave to soak
for 15 minutes. Place bowl in a
saucepan of simmering water, and
leave until gelatine has dissolved.
Heat stock in pan. Add gelatine.
Allow to cool, and stir in sherry.
Make a lattice of pimento on top of
mackerel pâté. Carefully pour over
aspic to just cover pimento. Chill
in refrigerator.

**Smoked Mackerel Pâté (right)
and Salmon Pâté (bottom).**

Fruit and Vegetables

Stuffed Radicchio

PREPARATION TIME: 10 minutes

COOKING TIME: 5 minutes

SERVES: 4 people

1 radicchio (8 good whole leaves; the
  rest finely chopped)
60g (2oz) rice, cooked
1 tbsp chopped parsley
200g (7oz) can tuna fish, drained
2 tbsps capers
5ml (1 tsp) lemon juice
30ml (2 tbsps) double cream,
  whipped
30ml (2 tbsps) vermouth or dry sherry
Salt
Pepper

Garnish
Lemon slices
Parsley

Flake tuna fish and mix with rice,
chopped radicchio, parsley, lemon
juice, capers, double cream and
wine and salt and pepper to taste.
Divide mixture evenly between
4 whole radicchio leaves and place
remaining 4 on top. Serve garnished
with lemon slices and parsley.

Asparagus with Hollandaise Sauce

PREPARATION TIME: 10 minutes

COOKING TIME: 30 minutes

SERVES: 4 people

20-32 asparagus spears
Nut of butter
Salt

Hollandaise Sauce
3 egg yolks
5ml (1 tsp) lemon juice if desired
175g (6oz) unsalted butter, diced
15ml (1 tbsp) wine vinegar
Salt
White pepper

Wash and trim asparagus stalks,
removing woody ends where
necessary. Place in a large, shallow
pan or large saucepan of boiling
salted water. Add nut of butter and
allow to simmer gently until tender
– about 10-15 minutes. If size of
spears varies greatly, add thicker
ones first so that they will all be
ready together. Drain. Meanwhile,
half-fill bottom half of double
saucepan with boiling water. Place
egg yolks and wine vinegar in top
half of double saucepan. Whisk
together until well mixed. Place
over bottom of saucepan and heat
gently, keeping water hot, but not
boiling. Stir until yolks are smooth.
Whisk in small pieces of butter, a
few at a time, until all butter has
been absorbed. Whisk sauce until
thick and creamy. Season with salt
and white pepper to taste and add
lemon juice if desired. Serve
asparagus spears with warm
Hollandaise sauce.

**This page: Stuffed Raddichio
(top) and Asparagus with
Hollandaise Sauce (bottom).**

**Facing page: Guacamole (top)
and Chicken Liver Pâté
(bottom).**

Tomato and Pepper Frostie

PREPARATION TIME:
15 minutes, plus freezing time

SERVES: 4 people

115ml (4 fl oz) can tomato juice
Juice of 1 lemon
6 ice cubes
5ml (1 tsp) Worcestershire sauce
½ small green pepper
½ small red pepper

Garnish
4 tomato flowers

Crush ice. Put tomato juice, lemon juice, ice and Worcestershire sauce in blender. Blend together. Put into ice-trays and place in freezer for ½ hour or until half-frozen. Meanwhile, remove core and seeds from peppers and dice finely. Remove tomato ice from freezer and transfer to a bowl, breaking up with the back of a fork. Mix in peppers. Re-freeze for a further 2 hours, stirring occasionally. For a garnish, make tomato flowers. Peel tomatoes (drop into boiling water; count to ten slowly; then rinse in cold water; remove skins). Starting at one end, with a sharp knife slice a continuous strip around the tomato. Form into a rose shape. Serve on top of tomato and pepper frostie.

Pepper Appetiser (left),
Aubergine Appetiser (bottom)
and Tomato and Pepper
Frostie (facing page).

Onion-Egg-Tomato Bake

PREPARATION TIME: 15 minutes

COOKING TIME: 20 minutes

OVEN TEMPERATURE:
200°C, 400°F, Gas Mark 6

SERVES: 4 people

4 eggs, hard boiled
2 medium onions, peeled and sliced
60g (2oz) butter or margarine
30g (1oz) flour
150ml (¼ pint) milk
2 tomatoes, skinned and sliced thinly
1 tbsp breadcrumbs
1 tbsp freshly grated Parmesan cheese
Salt
Pepper

Garnish
Parsley

Melt butter in pan. Add onions and fry over gentle heat until softened but not coloured. Remove with a slotted spoon and set aside. Stir in flour and cook for 1 minute. Remove from heat and gradually stir in milk. Beat well and return to heat. Cook for 3 minutes, stirring continuously. Add onions and plenty of seasoning to counteract the sweetness of the onions. Cut eggs in half. Remove yolks, sieve and set aside. Rinse and slice egg whites. Place in the bottom of an ovenproof dish. Cover with onion mixture, then with a layer of sliced tomatoes. Mix together egg yolk, breadcrumbs and Parmesan cheese. Sprinkle over top and place in a hot oven until golden on top. Garnish with parsley.

Pepper Appetiser

PREPARATION TIME: 15 minutes

COOKING TIME: 1 hour 15 minutes

SERVES: 4 people

1 green pepper
1 red pepper
2 tomatoes
2 onions
60ml (4 tbsps) white vinegar
30ml (2 tbsps) oil
Salt

Remove core and seeds from peppers and slice lengthways. Peel and slice onions and tomatoes. Heat oil in a large suacepan. Add vegetables and salt to taste and simmer, covered, for 1 hour, stirring occasionally. Remove lid and add vinegar, and simmer for a further 15 minutes. Allow to cool, and chill in refrigerator.

Aubergine Appetiser

PREPARATION TIME: 15 minutes

COOKING TIME: 20 minutes

SERVES: 4 people

1 large aubergine
2 ripe tomatoes, peeled, seeds removed, and chopped
2 cloves garlic, crushed
60ml (4 tbsps) oil
1 tbsp tomato purée
60ml (4 tbsps) water
Salt
Pepper

Cut aubergine lengthwise into strips 1cm x 6cm (¼" x 2½"). Heat oil in pan until hot. Add aubergine and cook for 5 minutes or until cooked. Remove from pan with slotted spoon. Add extra oil as necessary and heat. Fry garlic for 30 seconds. Add tomatoes, tomato purée, salt and pepper, and water and cook for 10 minutes or until sauce is thick. Add aubergine and stir together. Adjust seasoning and cook for a further 5 minutes. Serve hot or cold.

Avocado Lemon Ring

PREPARATION TIME:
10 minutes, plus setting time

SERVES: 4 people

2 avocado pears
1 pkt lemon jelly
150ml (¼ pint) hot water
1 lemon
10ml (2 tsps) Worcestershire sauce
150ml (¼ pint) double cream
Salt

Garnish
Slices of lemon
Watercress

Dissolve the jelly in hot water and leave to cool. Grate finely the rind of the lemon, and squeeze and strain the juice. Peel the avocado pears and remove the pips. Mash well with a fork. Pour on the cooled jelly and whisk or blend. Add lemon juice, rind, Worcestershire sauce, a pinch of salt and cream, and mix well. Pour into dampened ring mould and leave to set. Turn out to serve and garnish with slices of lemon and watercress in centre.

Grilled Grapefruit

PREPARATION TIME: 45 minutes

COOKING TIME: 10 minutes

SERVES: 4 people

2 grapefruit
60g (2oz) brown sugar
30ml (2 tbsps) Grand Marnier or Cointreau liqueur
1 tbsp clear honey

Garnish
Fresh or maraschino cherries
Fresh mint leaf

Cut grapefruit in half around equators. With a grapefruit knife or sharp knife, cut around edge between flesh of fruit and pith. Then cut down between each segment, removing skin from flesh. Take core between finger and thumb and pull out, removing with skin. Remove any pips. Pour excess juice into bowl. Sprinkle each grapefruit half with sugar and pour over liqueur. Leave to stand for 30 minutes. Meanwhile, mix together honey and grapefruit juice. Pre-heat grill. Pour over honey/grapefruit juice mixture and grill until just browning on top. Trim away any burnt skin and garnish with a cherry and mint leaf.

Broccoli Timbales

PREPARATION TIME: 10 minutes

COOKING TIME: 30 minutes

OVEN TEMPERATURE:
190°C, 375°F, Gas Mark 5

SERVES: 4 people

4 broccoli florets
30g (1oz) butter or margarine
30g (1oz) plain flour
300ml (½ pint) milk
1 tsp ground nutmeg
2 eggs, beaten
Salt
Pepper

Blanch broccoli in boiling salted water for 3 minutes. Drain and refresh under cold water. Drain and set aside. Melt butter in pan. Stir in flour and nutmeg and cook for 1 minute. Remove from heat and stir in milk gradually. Return to heat and bring to the boil, stirring continuously. Cook for 3 minutes. Add salt and white pepper to taste and beat well. Set aside to cool. Butter 4 ramekin dishes. Place a floret of broccoli in each dish with stem pointing upwards. Beat eggs into cooled white sauce, and pour into each ramekin dish. Place ramekins in a shallow baking tin. Pour boiling water into tin to a depth of 2.5cm (1"). Bake in a pre-heated oven for 15 minutes, or until just setting. Remove from oven and turn out onto individual plates. Serve immediately.

Onion-Egg-Tomato Bake (right) and Broccoli Timbales (bottom).

Fanned Avocado Salad with Prawn and Tomato Dressing

PREPARATION TIME: 20 minutes

SERVES: 4 people

2 ripe avocados
Juice of ½ lemon or 1 lime
225g (8oz) prawns or shrimps,
  shelled and de-veined
3 tbsps mayonnaise
1 tbsp tomato purée
15ml (1 tbsp) single cream
Salt
Pepper

Garnish
Lemon or lime rings
Lettuce leaves

Mix together mayonnaise, tomato purée, cream and salt and pepper to taste. Mix prawns with 2 tbsps mayonnaise mixture and set aside. Cut avocados in half. Remove pips and peel back and remove skin. Slice down through flesh 5 or 6 times. Keep thin end intact. Place on lettuce leaves on serving dishes and press down so that avocado fans out. Sprinkle over lemon or lime juice to prevent flesh browning. Place prawns at side of dish, around avocado. Garnish with lemon or lime rings.

Stuffed Mushrooms

PREPARATION TIME: 15 minutes

COOKING TIME: 20 minutes

OVEN TEMPERATURE:
200°C, 400°F, Gas Mark 6

SERVES: 4 people

4 large or 8 medium flat or cap
  mushrooms, stalks discarded
15ml (1 tbsp) olive oil
2 medium onions, peeled and
  chopped finely
225g (8oz) spinach, trimmed, cooked
  and chopped finely
2 tbsps fresh white breadcrumbs
60g (2oz) butter or margarine
4 cloves garlic, crushed
1 egg, beaten
½ tsp nutmeg
Salt
Pepper

Garnish
1 tbsp chopped parsley

Heat butter in pan. Add garlic, onion and nutmeg and fry gently until onion has softened. Remove from pan and set aside to cool.

Meanwhile, heat oil in pan and sauté mushrooms on both sides until lightly browned. Place underside-up in a shallow oven-proof dish. Mix together onion mixture, spinach, breadcrumbs, and salt and freshly ground black pepper to taste. Stir in beaten egg. Cover each mushroom cap with the mixture, shaping neatly. Cover with aluminium foil and bake in a hot oven for 10 minutes. Serve immediately, garnished with chopped parsley.

**This page: Grilled Grapefruit (top) and Avocado Lemon Ring (bottom).
Facing page: Stuffed Mushrooms (top) and Fanned Avocado Salad with Prawn and Tomato Dressing (bottom).**

Melon Balls in Mulled Wine

PREPARATION TIME: 1 hour

COOKING TIME: 10 minutes

SERVES: 4 people

1 melon
½ bottle red wine
2 cinnamon sticks
4 cloves
3 blades mace
Juice and pared rind of 1 orange
1 tsp freshly grated nutmeg
60g (2oz) granulated sugar

Put wine, orange juice and rind, spices and sugar into a pan and heat gently. Do not allow to boil. When hot, remove from heat and leave to infuse for an hour. Strain. Meanwhile, cut melon in half and scrape out pips. Then make melon balls with a melon-ball scoop, or cut into chunks. Place in individual serving dishes and pour over mulled wine.

Orange, Grapefruit and Mint Salad

PREPARATION TIME:
20 minutes, plus chilling time

SERVES: 4 people

2 grapefruit
3 oranges
1 tbsp granulated sugar
4 sprigs of mint

Garnish
Mint sprig

Cut the peel and pith off the grapefruit and oranges. Cut carefully inside the skin of each segment to remove each section of flesh. When skin only is left, squeeze to extract juices over a pan. Repeat with all fruit. Add sugar to pan and

Orange, Grapefruit and Mint Salad (right) and Melon Balls in Mulled Wine (inset below).

set over a gentle heat until sugar dissolves. Cool. Meanwhile, arrange orange and grapefruit segments alternating in dish. Chop mint finely and add to fruit syrup. Carefully spoon syrup over fruit. Chill. Garnish with a sprig of mint.

Pastries and Crêpes

Chicken Vol-au-Vents

PREPARATION TIME:	30 minutes
COOKING TIME:	30 minutes
OVEN TEMPERATURE:	210°C, 425°F, Gas Mark 7
SERVES:	4 people

225g (8oz) frozen puff pastry, thawed
1 egg, beaten

Filling
60g (2oz) butter or margarine
45g (1½oz) flour
300ml (½ pint) milk
Salt
Pepper
4 chicken breasts, cooked and
     shredded
1 tbsp chopped parsley
6 peppercorns
2 parsley stalks
Slice of onion
Half a bay leaf

On a lightly floured board roll out pastry to about 1cm (¼") thick. Using a 7.5cm (3") fluted pastry-cutter, cut out pastry. With a 5cm (2") fluted pastry-cutter mark centre of each, being careful not to cut right through. Brush with beaten egg, being careful not to get any down sides or in groove made by 5cm (2") cutter, as this will prevent rising. Place on a dampened baking tray and chill in refrigerator for 15 minutes. Make pattern on outer edge with back of knife if desired. Bake in a hot oven until golden brown. Remove from oven and gently prise off centre cap. Remove any soft pastry from inside. Return to oven for 1 minute to dry out. To help prevent pastry from toppling over, 4 cocktail sticks may be placed at equal intervals around outside circle and removed after cooking. Heat milk with peppercorns, parsley stalks, onion and ½ bay leaf until just simmering. Remove from heat, cover and leave to cool for 7 minutes. Strain. Melt butter in pan; stir in flour and cook for 1 minute. Remove from heat and gradually stir in infused milk. Return to heat, bring to the boil and cook for 3 minutes, stirring continuously. Add salt and pepper to taste. Stir in shredded chicken and parsley. Fill vol-au-vent cases with hot chicken filling. Place lids on top at an angle. Serve hot.

Prawn Vol-au-Vents

PREPARATION TIME:	30 minutes
COOKING TIME:	30 minutes
OVEN TEMPERATURE:	210°C, 425°F, Gas Mark 7
SERVES:	4 people

225g (8oz) frozen puff pastry, thawed
1 egg, beaten

Filling
60g (2oz) butter or margarine
45g (1½oz) flour
300ml (½ pint) chicken stock
Salt
Pepper
225g (8oz) prawns or shrimps,
     shelled and de-veined
15ml (1 tbsp) tarragon vinegar or
     lemon juice
1 tsp tomato purée
Pinch of sugar

On a lightly floured board, roll out pastry to about 1cm (¼") thick. Using a 7.5cm (3") fluted pastry-cutter, cut out pastry. With a 5cm (2") fluted pastry-cutter mark the centre of each, being careful not to cut right through. Brush with beaten egg, being careful not to get any down sides or in groove made

Roquefort Tartlets (top) and Cheese Puffs (bottom).

Facing page: Chicken Vol-au-Vents (top) and Prawn Vol-au-Vents (bottom).

by 5cm (2") cutter, as this will prevent rising. Place on a dampened baking tray and chill in refrigerator for 15 minutes. Make pattern on outer circle with back of knife if desired. Bake in a hot oven until golden brown. Remove from oven and gently prise off centre cap. Remove any soft pastry from inside and return to oven for 1 minute to dry out. To help prevent pastry from toppling over, 4 cocktail sticks may be placed at equal intervals around outside circle, and removed after cooking. Melt butter in pan. Stir in flour and cook for 1 minute. Remove from heat and gradually stir in chicken stock. Return to heat, bring to the boil, and cook for 3 minutes, stirring continuously. Stir in prawns, tomato purée, tarragon vinegar or lemon juice, sugar and salt and pepper to taste. Simmer for a further 3 minutes. Fill vol-au-vents with hot prawn filling. Place lids on top at an angle. Serve hot.

Mushroom Vol-au-Vents

PREPARATION TIME: 30 minutes	
COOKING TIME: 20 minutes	
OVEN TEMPERATURE: 210°C, 425°F, Gas Mark 7	
SERVES: 4 people	

225g (8oz) frozen puff pastry, thawed
1 egg, beaten

Filling
60g (2oz) butter or margarine
45g (1½oz) flour
300ml (½ pint) chicken stock
Salt
Pepper
225g (8oz) cup or flat mushrooms
1 onion, peeled and chopped finely
30ml (2 tbsps) cream
1 tsp chopped parsley

Garnish
Chopped parsley

On a lightly floured board roll out pastry to about 1cm (¼") thick. Using a 7.5cm (3") fluted pastry-cutter, cut out pastry. With a 5cm (2") fluted pastry-cutter mark centre of each, being careful not to cut right through. Brush with beaten egg, being careful not to get any down sides or in groove made by 5cm (2") cutter, as this will prevent rising. Place on a dampened baking tray and chill in refrigerator for 15 minutes. Make pattern on outer circle with back of knife if desired. Bake in a hot oven until golden brown. Remove from oven and gently prise off centre cap. Remove any soft pastry from

inside, and return to oven for 1 minute to dry out. To help prevent pastry from toppling over, 4 cocktail sticks may be placed at equal intervals around outside circle and removed after cooking. Wash mushrooms. Chop half of them very finely, the remainder roughly. Melt butter in pan. Add roughly-chopped mushrooms and cook for 3 minutes. Remove with slotted spoon and set aside. Add onion to pan and, after a minute, finely chopped mushrooms. Cook for 4 minutes. Stir in flour and cook for 1 minute. Remove from heat and gradually stir in chicken stock. Return to heat, bring to the boil and cook for 3 minutes, stirring continuously. Add cream, rough-chopped mushrooms, parsley and salt and pepper and simmer for 1 minute. Fill vol-au-vents with hot mushroom filling. Sprinkle with parsley and place lids on top at an angle. Serve hot.

Quiche Lorraine

PREPARATION TIME: 30 minutes	
COOKING TIME: 45 minutes	
OVEN TEMPERATURE: 190°C, 375°F, Gas Mark 5	
SERVES: 6 people	

Pastry
175g (6oz) plain flour
Pinch of salt
90g (3oz) butter or margarine
30g (1oz) lard
Cold water

Filling
15g (½oz) butter or margarine
2 eggs, beaten
30g (1oz) Gruyère or Cheddar cheese, grated
150ml (¼ pint) single cream
10 spring onions, cut into 5cm (2") slices
½ tsp dried mustard
60g (2oz) streaky bacon, diced
Salt
Pepper

Sift flour and salt into a bowl. Cut cold fat into small pieces and drop into flour. With 2 round-ended knives cut fat into flour. When well cut in, use fingers to rub in completely. Mix to a firm but pliable dough with cold water. Knead on a lightly floured board until smooth. Chill for 15 minutes in the refrigerator. Roll out on a lightly floured board and line a 24cm (9½") flan ring. Melt butter in frying pan and add bacon and spring onions, and fry gently until turning a light golden-brown

colour. Place in a bowl. Add beaten eggs, cheese, cream, mustard and salt and pepper to taste, and stir well. Pour into prepared pastry case. Bake in oven for 20-25 minutes until golden brown. Serve hot or cold.

Cheese Puffs

PREPARATION TIME: 20 minutes	
COOKING TIME: 20 minutes	
OVEN TEMPERATURES: 190°C, 375°F, Gas Mark 5 200°C, 400°F, Gas Mark 6	
SERVES: 4 people	

Pastry
115g (4oz) plain flour
Pinch of salt
90g (3oz) butter or margarine
225ml (8 fl oz) water
3 medium eggs, lightly beaten

Filling
75g (2½ oz) Gruyère cheese, grated
75g (2½ oz) Emmenthal cheese, grated
1 egg, beaten
10ml (2 tsps) kirsch
1 egg yolk, beaten, for glaze

Pre-set oven to 190°C or equivalent. Sift flour and salt onto a sheet of greaseproof paper. Place butter and water in pan over gentle heat. When butter has melted, bring to boil and straightaway add all flour. Beat well until mixture is smooth. Leave to cool. Add eggs gradually to mixture, beating well. Using a teaspoon or a piping bag with a plain nozzle, shape mixture into balls about the size of golf balls onto a lightly greased baking tray. Place in oven and increase heat to 200°C or equivalent. Bake for 10 minutes until firm on outside. Remove from oven and make a hole in bottom or side. Mix together cheese, egg and kirsch. Pipe in cheese mixture and brush tops with egg-yolk. Return to oven for 5 minutes. Serve immediately.

Roquefort Tartlets

PREPARATION TIME: 30 minutes	
COOKING TIME: 20 minutes	
OVEN TEMPERATURE: 190°C, 375°F, Gas Mark 5	
SERVES: 4 people	

Pastry
175g (6oz) plain flour
Pinch of salt
90g (3oz) butter or margarine
30g (1oz) lard
Cold water

Filling
115g (4oz) Roquefort cheese
115g (4oz) cream cheese
30ml (2 tbsps) single cream
2 eggs, lightly beaten

Sift salt and flour into a bowl. Cut cold fat into small pieces and drop into flour. With 2 round-ended knives cut fat into flour. When well cut in, use fingers to rub in completely. Mix to a firm but pliable dough with cold water. Knead on a lightly floured board until smooth. Chill for 15 minutes in the refrigerator. Meanwhile, gently melt together Roquefort cheese and cream cheese in a pan, stirring continuously. When melted, set aside to cool. Mix together cream and beaten eggs, and add to cheese mixture, stirring well. Roll out dough on a lightly floured board. Using a 7.5cm (3") fluted pastry-cutter, cut out rounds of pastry. Line a patty tin. Prick bottom of pastry cases with a fork. Spoon mixture into individual pastry cases and bake in the oven for about 15 minutes until golden brown.

Chicken and Ham Crêpes

PREPARATION TIME: 5 minutes	
COOKING TIME: 30 minutes	
OVEN TEMPERATURE: 200°C, 400°F, Gas Mark 6	
SERVES: 4-6 people	

Crêpe Batter
115g (4oz) plain flour
Pinch of salt
2 medium eggs
300ml (½ pint) milk
15ml (1 tbsp) olive oil or vegetable oil
Oil to grease pan

Filling
2 chicken breasts, cooked and shredded
2 slices ham, shredded
1 tsp French mustard
2 tbsps grated Cheddar or Gruyère cheese
60g (2oz) butter or margarine
45g (1½oz) flour
300ml (½ pint) milk
Salt
Pepper

Garnish
Parsley

Sift flour and salt into a bowl. Make a well in the centre and drop in eggs. Start to mix in eggs gradually, taking in flour around edges. When becoming stiff, add a little milk until all flour has been incorporated. Beat to a smooth batter, then add remaining milk. Stir in oil. Cover bowl, and leave in a cool place for 30 minutes. Heat small frying pan, or 19cm (7″) crêpe pan. Wipe over with oil. When hot, add enough batter mixture to cover base of pan when rolled. Pour off any excess batter. When brown on underside, loosen and turn over with a palette-knife, and brown on other side. Pile on a plate and cover with a clean tea-towel until needed. Melt butter in pan. Stir in flour and cook for 1 minute. Remove from heat and gradually stir in milk. Return to heat, bring to the boil, and cook for 3 minutes, stirring continuously. Add cheese, chicken, ham and French mustard, and salt and pepper and stir until heated through. Do not re-boil. Divide the mixture evenly between the pancakes and roll up or fold into triangles. Place in a baking dish and cover with aluminium foil. Heat in a hot oven for 10 minutes. Garnish with parsley. Serve immediately.

Mushroom Vol-au-Vents (left) and Quiche Lorraine (bottom).

Seafood Crêpes

PREPARATION TIME: 45 minutes

COOKING TIME: 20 minutes

OVEN TEMPERATURE: 200°C, 400°F, Gas Mark 6

SERVES: 4-6 people

Crêpe Batter
115g (4oz) plain flour
Pinch of salt
2 medium eggs
300ml (½ pint) milk
15ml (1 tbsp) olive oil or vegetable oil
Oil to grease pan

Filling
115g (4oz) prawns or shrimps, peeled and de-veined
2 scallops, cleaned and sliced

115g (4oz) white fish fillets
Squeeze of lemon juice
15ml (1 tbsp) lemon juice
8 spring onions, sliced

60g (2oz) butter or margarine
45g (1½oz) flour
300ml (½ pint) milk
Salt
Pepper

Sift flour and salt into a bowl. Make a well in the centre and drop in eggs. Start to mix in eggs gradually, taking in flour around edges. When becoming stiff, add a little milk until all flour has been incorporated. Beat to a smooth batter, then add remaining milk. Stir in oil. Cover bowl and leave in a cool place for 30 minutes. Heat

small frying pan or 19cm (7″) crêpe pan. Wipe over with oil. When hot, add enough batter mixture to cover base of pan when rolled. Pour off any excess batter. When brown on underside, loosen and turn over with a palette-knife and brown on other side. Pile on a plate and cover with a clean tea-towel until needed. Poach scallops and fish in water with a squeeze of lemon juice for 4 minutes or until cooked through. Melt butter in pan. Add spring onions and cook for 3 minutes. Remove with slotted spoon and set aside. Stir in the flour and cook for 1 minute. Remove from heat and gradually stir in milk. Return to heat, bring to the boil, and cook for 3 minutes, stirring continuously. Add spring

onions, seafood and lemon juice, and salt and pepper and stir well until heated through. Do not re-boil. Divide the mixture evenly between the pancakes and roll up or fold into triangles. Place in a baking dish and cover with aluminium foil. Heat in a hot oven for 10 minutes. Serve immediately.

This page: Egg and Fish Flan.

Facing page: Chicken and Ham Crêpes (top) and Seafood Crêpes (bottom).

Egg and Fish Flan

| **PREPARATION TIME:** 30 minutes |
| **COOKING TIME:** 45 minutes |
| **OVEN TEMPERATURE:** 190°C, 375°F, Gas Mark 5 |
| **SERVES:** 6 people |

Pastry
175g (6oz) plain flour
Pinch of salt
90g (3oz) butter or margarine
30g (1oz) lard
Cold water

Filling
2 eggs, beaten
225g (8oz) white fish fillets
45g (1½oz) can anchovy fillets,
  drained
10 black olives, halved and pips
  removed
30ml (2 tbsps) single cream
15ml (1 tbsp) lemon juice
1 bay leaf
6 peppercorns
Parsley stalks
Slice of onion
300ml (½ pint) cold water
1 onion peeled and chopped
60g (2oz) butter
45g (1½oz) flour
Salt
Pepper

Poach fish in 300ml (½ pint) water, with lemon juice, peppercorns, bay leaf, slice of onion and parsley stalks, for 10 minutes or until just cooked. Remove from poaching liquid. Strain, reserving liquid, and cool. Melt butter in pan. Add onion and fry gently until softened. Stir in flour and cook for 1 minute. Draw off heat and gradually stir in reserved liquid, stirring continuously. Add salt and pepper to taste. Return to heat and cook for 3 minutes. Set aside to cool. Sift salt and flour into a bowl. Cut cold fat into small pieces and drop into flour. With 2 round-ended knives, cut fat into flour. When well cut in, use fingers to rub in completely. Mix to a firm but pliable dough with cold water. Knead on a lightly floured board until smooth. Chill for 15 minutes in the refrigerator. Roll out on a lightly floured board and line a 24cm (9½″) flan ring. Flake fish and place in bottom of prepared pastry case. Stir cream into lightly beaten egg. Add mixture to sauce gradually, and pour over fish. Arrange anchovy fillets in a lattice over top, with a piece of olive in the centre of each diamond. Bake in oven for 20-25 minutes until golden brown. Serve hot or cold.

Fish and Seafood

Trout in Aspic

PREPARATION TIME: 40 minutes
COOKING TIME: 30 minutes
SERVES: 4 people

4 small fresh trout, cleaned
20ml (4 tsps) lemon juice
Nut of butter
Salt
Pepper

Aspic
300ml (½ pint) clear, strained
  chicken stock
2 tsps powdered gelatine
30ml (2 tbsps) dry sherry
30ml (2 tbsps) cold water or 1 packet
  commercial aspic, used as directed

Decoration
1 carrot
4 stuffed olives
Chives

Garnish
Parsley

Preheat grill. Divide lemon juice
and butter equally and place in the
cavity of each trout. Grill carefully
until cooked – about 10-15 minutes
on each side. Set aside to cool.
Carefully remove skin from body of
fish. Chill in refrigerator.
Sprinkle gelatine over a small bowl
containing 15-30ml (1-2 tbsps) of
cold water, and leave to soak for
15 minutes. Place bowl in a
saucepan of simmering water and
leave until gelatine has dissolved.
Heat stock in pan. Add gelatine.
Allow to cool, and stir in sherry.
Make a flower design on the side of
each fish with sliced carrot cut into
petals, with sliced, stuffed olives as
the centre of each flower and chives
for the stems. When aspic is cool,
carefully brush or pour over a thin
coating. Repeat if necessary, and
reheat aspic slightly if it is setting in
the pan. Refrigerate fish until ready
for serving. Garnish with parsley.

Dressed Crab

PREPARATION TIME: 45 minutes
SERVES: 4 people

1 large or 2 small cooked crabs
1 tsp French mustard
1 tsp horseradish

1 tbsp fresh breadcrumbs
1 egg, hard boiled
1 tbsp chopped parsley
Salt
Pepper

Garnish
Watercress

Take crab and twist off large claws.
Twist off small claws and set aside
for decoration. Grasp under-body
and pull away from main shell.
Remove and discard feathery gills,
and any green matter. Discard
stomach sac that lies in top part of
body. Set body aside. Scrape out all
brown and white meat from main
shell and place in separate bowls.
Place a cloth over shell and with a
little pressure, break along natural
indentation. Scrub shell inside and
outside, dry thoroughly and rub
with oil. Set aside. Break large

claws, remove all white meat and
place it in bowl. Cut main body in
half and pick out white and dark
meat. Place in respective bowls.
Cream the dark meat and mix with

This page: Dressed Crab.

Facing page: Trout in Aspic.

breadcrumbs. Add French mustard, horseradish and salt and pepper, a little at a time, to desired taste. Place white meat into cavity in prepared shell. Part meat down centre and spoon in dark meat mixture.

Cut egg in half. Remove yolk and push through a sieve. Rinse egg white, and slice.

Sprinkle dark meat mixture with sieved egg yolk. Place a border of egg white either side of yolk. Sprinkle a line of parsley between egg white and egg yolk.

On a serving dish, set out crab claws. Place dressed crab on top. Garnish with watercress and serve with buttered brown bread if desired.

Fish in Lime and Coconut

PREPARATION TIME:
20 minutes, plus marinating time

SERVES: 4 people

450g (1lb) white fish fillets
1 cup lime juice
1 cup desiccated coconut
2 cups milk
8 spring onions
1 green chilli
Salt

Garnish
Slices of lime

Heat milk to boiling point. Pour over desiccated coconut and leave until cool. Put into a sieve and squeeze out coconut cream. Discard pulp. Trim and slice spring onions. Remove seeds from chilli and slice finely. Blanch in boiling water for 2 minutes. Rinse in cold water and drain. Cut fish into bite-size pieces, sprinkle with salt, and leave a few minutes. Place in a deep bowl, and cover completely with lime juice. Leave 2-3 hours until fish is white, turning occasionally. Strain off lime juice and squeeze the flesh gently to soak the juice right through. Pour over coconut cream with chilli and spring onions. Toss. Chill well. Serve garnished with lime slices.

Fish Timbales with Lemon Sauce

PREPARATION TIME: 10 minutes

COOKING TIME: 45 minutes

OVEN TEMPERATURE:
190°C, 375°F, Gas Mark 5

SERVES: 4 people

225g (8oz) cod, or other whitefish,
   fillets
30g (1oz) butter or margarine
30g (1oz) plain flour
150ml (¼ pint) milk
Salt
Pepper
1 large egg
30ml (2 tbsps) lemon juice

Lemon Sauce
1½ cups cream
¼ cup lemon juice
1 tsp cornflour
1 tbsp French mustard
1 tbsp chopped sorrel

Garnish
Dill

Put cod in pan. Cover with water and simmer for 10 minutes. Remove skin and bones from fish. Melt butter in pan. Bring to boil and simmer for 3 minutes. Beat fish and sauce together. Add egg, lemon juice, and salt and pepper to taste. Butter 4 ramekin dishes and put a disc of buttered greaseproof paper in the base of each. Spoon in fish mixture. Place ramekins in a shallow baking tin. Pour boiling water into tin to a depth of 2.5cm (1"). Bake in a pre-heated oven for 20 minutes. Meanwhile, mix cream with cornflour in a small pan, add lemon juice and heat to boiling point. Simmer for 3 minutes and set aside. Add 1 tbsp French mustard and 1 tbsp of sorrel, if available. Turn each timbale out on a plate and serve with lemon sauce. Garnish with dill.

Sardines

PREPARATION TIME: 20 minutes

COOKING TIME: 25 minutes

OVEN TEMPERATURE:
220°C, 425°F, Gas Mark 7

SERVES: 4 people

12 fresh or frozen sardines
115g (4oz) mushrooms, chopped
   finely
2 shallots, peeled and chopped finely
2 cloves garlic, crushed

30g (1oz) butter or margarine
60g (2oz) fresh breadcrumbs
15ml (1 tbsp) lemon juice
2 tbsps chopped parsley
Pinch of freshly grated nutmeg
Salt
Pepper

Garnish
Lemon slices
Cress

Wash sardines and remove any scales. Cut sardines along stomach, being careful not to cut through back. Remove head, gills and stomach sac. Remove backbone from head end to tail. Remove tail. Wash and pat dry with absorbent paper. Heat butter in pan. Add garlic, shallots and mushrooms and fry for 5 minutes. Remove from heat and add breadcrumbs, parsley,

This page: **Coquilles St Jacques (top) and Rollmops with Apple Mayonnaise. Facing page: Fish Timbales with Lemon Sauce (top) and Sardines (bottom).**

lemon juice, nutmeg and salt and pepper to taste. Spread sardine fillets with the stuffing and close up. Place in a greased baking tin.

Bake in a hot oven for 15 minutes or until cooked. Garnish with lemon slices and cress, if desired, and serve hot or cold with buttered toast.

Crab and Prawn Cocktail

PREPARATION TIME: 15 minutes
SERVES: 4 people

60g (2oz) fresh crabmeat, flaked or 1 small can crabmeat, drained and flaked
115g (4oz) prawns or shrimps, shelled and de-veined
1 lettuce, rinsed and cut into shreds

Sauce
2 tbsps mayonnaise
5ml (1 tsp) lemon juice
1 tsp tomato purée
Salt
Pepper

In 4 individual glasses, place a bed of shredded lettuce. Mix together prawns and crabmeat. Divide mixture equally between the 4 glasses, alternating each spoonful of the prawn crab mixture with a small amount of shredded lettuce. Mix together the mayonnaise, lemon juice, tomato purée and salt and pepper to taste. Spoon over cocktail just before serving. Serve with buttered brown bread.

Salmon Mousse

PREPARATION TIME: 45 minutes
COOKING TIME: 15 minutes
SERVES: 4 people

185g (6½ oz) can red or pink salmon, drained
30g (1oz) butter or margarine
30g (1oz) flour
300ml (½ pint) milk
Salt
Pepper
60g (2oz) butter, creamed
1 tbsp whipped cream
1 tsp tomato purée
15ml (1 tbsp) sherry
1 dsp gelatine
45ml (3 tbsps) cold water

Garnish
Cucumber, sliced
Stuffed olive, for eye
Watercress

Melt butter in pan. Stir in flour and cook for 1 minute. Draw off heat and gradually stir in milk. Beat well. Return to heat and cook for 3 minutes, stirring continuously.

Season with salt and pepper to taste. Break up salmon with back of spoon. Add sauce gradually, then carefully stir in tomato purée, creamed butter, cream and sherry. Sprinkle gelatine into a small bowl with water. Leave to soak 15 minutes. Place bowl in a saucepan of hot water and simmer gently until gelatine has dissolved completely. Stir gelatine into mixture carefully. Turn into a lightly-oiled fish mould. Smooth surface and chill in refrigerator for 15 minutes or until firm. Turn out. Garnish with stuffed olive for eye, cucumber slices on body of fish, and watercress.

Rollmops with Apple Mayonnaise

PREPARATION TIME:
30 minutes, plus chilling time
COOKING TIME: 20 minutes
OVEN TEMPERATURE:
180°C, 350°F, Gas Mark 4
SERVES: 4 people

4 small or 2 large herrings
450ml (¾ pint) vinegar
6 peppercorns
1 bay leaf
3 medium onions, peeled and sliced
2 tbsps English mustard

Sauce
2 dessert apples
4 tbsps mayonnaise
2 tbsps soured cream
15ml (1 tbsp) lemon juice
Salt
Pepper

Garnish
Parsley

Preheat oven. Clean herrings and open out flat (if large, cut in half lengthways). Rinse and pat dry with absorbent paper. Pour vinegar into a saucepan with peppercorns, bay leaf and sliced onions. Simmer for 5 minutes and allow to cool. Spread mustard over flesh of the herrings. Drain onions and place on flesh of fish, and roll up. Secure with a wooden cocktail stick. Arrange in an ovenproof dish. Strain vinegar and pour over herrings. Cover and cook in oven for 10-15 minutes. Allow to cool. Meanwhile, mix together mayonnaise, lemon juice, soured cream and salt and pepper to taste. Peel and grate apples and add to mayonnaise mixture. Serve rollmops with apple mayonnaise, and garnished with parsley.

Herring and Apple Salad, with Soured Cream Sauce

PREPARATION TIME: 20 minutes
SERVES: 4 people

500ml (18 fl oz) bottle soused herrings, drained
3 medium-sized dessert apples, cored and diced
2 tsps horseradish
30ml (2 tbsps) cream
30ml (2 tbsps) soured cream
Salt
Freshly ground black pepper

Garnish
1 red apple, sliced

Rinse herrings thoroughly in cold water, and pat dry with absorbent paper. Cut fillets into small pieces and put into a dish with diced apples. Blend together horseradish, cream, soured cream, and salt and pepper. Pour over diced herrings and apple, and toss together gently. Line a dish with sliced red apple, and pile apple and herring salad in centre. Squeeze lemon juice over apples to prevent browning, if not being served immediately.

Coquilles St Jacques

PREPARATION TIME: 15 minutes
COOKING TIME: 20 minutes
SERVES: 4 people

225g (8oz) scallops
60ml (4 tbsps) white wine
300ml (½ pint) water
Slice of lemon
1 bay leaf
3 peppercorns
Slice of onion
Salt
Pepper
15ml (1 tbsp) single cream
45g (1½ oz) butter or margarine
30g (1oz) flour
2 tbsps fresh breadcrumbs
1 tbsp freshly grated Parmesan cheese

Place white wine, water, lemon slice, bay leaf, peppercorns and onion slice in a pan. Bring to the boil and reduce heat. Add scallops and simmer, covered, for 3-5 minutes, until scallops are cooked. Remove scallops with a draining spoon and allow to cool. Slice thinly. Strain cooking liquid and set aside to cool. Melt butter in pan. Stir in flour and cook for 1 minute. Draw off heat and gradually stir in cooled reserved liquid and salt and

pepper. Return to heat and cook gently for 3 minutes. Remove from heat and stir in cream. Place sliced scallops in individual dishes or cleaned scallop shells. Spoon over sauce and sprinkle with bread-crumbs and Parmesan cheese. Brown in a pre-heated grill. Serve immediately.

Fish Margherita

PREPARATION TIME: 15 minutes
COOKING TIME: 30 minutes
OVEN TEMPERATURE:
190°C, 375°F, Gas Mark 5
SERVES: 4 people

225g (8oz) white fish fillets, skinned and boned
1 red pepper, cored, seeds removed, and sliced
1 green pepper, cored, seeds removed, and sliced
1 onion, peeled and sliced
4 tomatoes, skinned, pips removed, and sliced
15g (½ oz) butter or margarine
2 cloves garlic, crushed
90ml (6 tbsps) water
15ml (1 tbsp) lemon juice
1 tsp tomato purée
½ tsp paprika
1 bay leaf
6 peppercorns
2 parsley stalks
Salt
Pepper

Place fish in an ovenproof dish with water, lemon juice, bay leaf, peppercorns and parsley stalks. Bake in oven for 15-20 minutes, until just cooked through. Remove fish and strain and reserve juices. Meanwhile, melt butter in pan. Add garlic and paprika and fry for 30 seconds. Add onion, and cover and fry gently for 5 minutes. Add peppers, tomato purée, fish liquor and salt and pepper. Cook a further 5 minutes, and add tomatoes and fish. Serve when fish has heated through.

Crab and Prawn Cocktail (top) and Herring and Apple Salad, with Soured Cream Sauce (above right).

Meat and Eggs

Cold Roast Beef and Horseradish Cream

PREPARATION TIME: 20 minutes

SERVES: 4 people

8 slices medium-rare roast beef
150ml (¼ pint) double cream
1 tbsp fresh grated horseradish
5ml (1 tsp) lemon juice
1 tsp sugar
Pinch of salt and pepper

Garnish
Lettuce
Spring onion flowers (trim and slice
*   lengthways, keep one end intact,*
*   and leave in cold water in*
*   refrigerator until curling)*
Cucumber

Whip cream and salt together until stiff. Add horseradish, sugar and lemon juice. Check seasoning, and add more salt and pepper if desired. Place one-eighth of each mixture at end of each slice of beef. Roll up in a cornet shape and serve on a bed of lettuce. Garnish with spring onion flowers and sliced cucumber.

Stuffed Eggs

PREPARATION TIME: 20 minutes

COOKING TIME: 15 minutes

SERVES: 4 people

6 medium eggs
15ml (1 tbsp) vinegar
1 small can of pink salmon
Paprika
30g (1oz) peas
30g (1oz) mushrooms
225g (8oz) cream cheese
Salt
Pepper

Garnish
Stuffed olive
Red pepper or tomato
Black olive

This page: Stuffed Eggs.

Facing page: Chicken Tongue Rolls (top) and Cold Roast Beef and Horseradish Cream (bottom).

Put eggs into a saucepan of gently boiling water with 15ml (1 tbsp) of vinegar and boil gently for 12 minutes. Rinse immediately in cold water. Remove shells carefully and keep eggs in cold water until ready to use. Cut boiled eggs in half and carefully remove yolks. Rinse whites. Push yolks through a sieve and put aside for fillings. Soften cream cheese by beating. Drain and flake salmon. Mix carefully with one-third of cream cheese. Add a pinch of paprika and salt and pepper to taste. Pipe or spoon filling into 4 egg whites. Garnish with half a stuffed olive.

Wash and trim mushrooms. Chop very finely and add to one-third of cream cheese. Add salt or pepper to taste. Pipe or spoon filling into 4 egg whites. Garnish with red pepper or tomato.

Cook peas until tender. Push through a sieve. Add yolk of eggs and one-third of cream cheese. Pipe or spoon filling into remaining 4 egg whites and garnish with a slice of black olive.

Chicken Tongue Rolls

PREPARATION TIME: 15 minutes	
COOKING TIME: 20 minutes	
SERVES: 4 people	

4 chicken legs
1 small can of tongue, sliced, or
   4 slices of tongue
2 tbsps grated Parmesan cheese
1 tbsp grated Gruyère or Cheddar
   cheese
1 tbsp chopped parsley
15ml (1 tbsp) oil
Salt
Pepper

Garnish
Parsley
Tomato

Remove bone carefully from chicken leg, keeping meat in one piece. Flatten out, and divide the tongue equally between each piece. Mix together grated cheeses, parsley and salt and pepper to taste. Place a tbsp of the mixture on each piece of chicken. Roll up chicken and tie each with string, 2 or 3 times. Heat oil in pan and fry chicken rolls gently for about 20 minutes, turning occasionally to cook evenly. Remove from heat and allow to cool. Cut off string and remove gently. Slice into rounds and serve garnished with parsley and tomato.

Egg Flower

PREPARATION TIME: 20 minutes	
COOKING TIME: 15 minutes	
SERVES: 4 people	

6 eggs
15ml (1 tbsp) vinegar
3 tbsps mayonnaise
15ml (1 tbsp) single cream
5ml (1 tsp) lemon juice (or to taste)
Salt
White pepper

Garnish
Watercress
Pinch of paprika

Fill a saucepan with water and 15ml (1 tbsp) of vinegar and bring to the boil. Reduce heat and simmer. Gently add eggs and cook for 12 minutes. Rinse under cold water to stop cooking. Crack and peel off shells and set eggs aside in a bowl of cold water. Mix together mayonnaise, cream, lemon juice and salt and white pepper to taste. Cut 4 eggs in half. Place yolk-side down in a circle on a serving dish. Cut remaining eggs in half and separate yolks from whites. Rinse whites and cut into shreds. Push yolks through a sieve and set aside. Pour mayonnaise over eggs on serving dish. Sprinkle egg white around outside. Sprinkle yolk on top towards the centre. Sprinkle with paprika. Finally garnish with a bunch of watercress in the centre.

Eggs baked in Tarragon Cream

PREPARATION TIME: 5 minutes	
COOKING TIME: 8 minutes	
OVEN TEMPERATURE: 180°C, 350°F, Gas Mark 4	
SERVES: 4 people	

4 large eggs
Nut of butter
60ml (4 tbsps) cream
1 tbsp chopped tarragon
Salt
Pepper

Butter individual oven-proof ramekin dishes. Break an egg into each dish. Add chopped tarragon, and salt and pepper to cream and mix well. Add 15ml (1 tbsp) of cream mixture to each ramekin. Place ramekins on a baking sheet in a pre-heated oven until set, about 6-8 minutes. Serve hot.

Eggs baked in Tarragon
Cream (left) and Egg Flower
(below).

Glossary

Arrowroot. Used for thickening sauces. Ground root of American plant of the same name.

Aspic. Clear jelly made with clarified stock of meat, fish or chicken and set with gelatine.

Bain-Marie. A vessel of hot water in which a smaller pan is placed for cooking contents, or to keep food warm. Gives a moist, hot atmosphere.

Blanch. Normally carried out to remove a strong taste.

Bouquet Garni. A faggot of herbs – usually consisting of a bay leaf, a sprig of thyme and a few parsley stalks tied together. Removed after cooking.

Clarified Butter. Ordinary butter rid of its impurities. When ordinary butter is heated, the top surface is skimmed clean, and when the sediment constituting milk solids has settled to the bottom, the golden liquid that is poured off is now clarified. With a higher burning point than most other oils, it is ideal for sautéing. It also keeps longer than ordinary butter and hence is ideal for sealing pâtés.

Cornflour. A fine, white maize flour used for thickening sauces.

Court Bouillon. A quickly made vegetable stock generally made from carrots, onions, cloves, peppercorns and a bouquet garni. It is usually lightly acidulated with vinegar or lemon juice (15ml [1 tbsp] to 600ml [1 pint] of water). It is used for poaching fish, and often strained and used in accompanying sauce.

Croûtons. Cubes of bread fried in fat until golden brown, drained, often salted, and served in soups.

Dice. Cut into small cubes.

Gelatine. Jelly used for setting that melts in hot liquids and sets when cold.

Infuse. To steep herbs or ingredients in liquid to extract flavours.

Sauté. To fry quickly over high temperature, in hot fat. Sautéing meat browns and seals in the juices before longer, slower cooking takes place.

Simmer. Cook just below boiling point.

Slake. Mix with a small quantity of liquid before adding to a liquid for thickening.

Strain. Separate liquids from solids by passing through a sieve.

Mushroom Soup (top), Smoked Mackerel Pâté (above), Chicken Liver Pâté (right) and Fish Margherita (top right).

Index